CUSTOMER SERVICE?

RECOGNIZING, EDUCATING, AND PROMOTING...

I0469455

Dr. Rae Pearson

"E-Diva"

TABLE OF CONTENTS

Introduction

There's no doubt about it, times have changed in the business world, with new tools like e-mail, texting, video conferencing and even "tweeting" dominating the corporate culture.

But there is one constant – the telephone. It's still a critical part of the U.S. work day.

The phone's business mission hasn't changed over the years – employees use it to communicate with clients, co-workers, and other companies, all people you may never see, yet who are critical to the success of your business.

The telephone also continues to be a powerful tool. After all, every call into your business is a call for an opportunity to help or hurt your bottom line, and sometimes all it takes are a few simple words to change a bad experience into a good experience.

"CUSTOMER SERVICE! RECOGNIZING, EDUCATING, AND PROMOTING..." will guide you through the essential steps to ensure that you maximize the impact of every telephone call you take – and make – on behalf of your employer.

Q. How has the economic downturn affected customer service?

A. The good news is that the economic downturn has made more companies recognize that it takes a lot more money to try to get new customers than to maintain current customers. And in a bad economy, companies really want to keep their customers satisfied. The bad news is, in an economic downturn, when companies need to cut expenses, customer service is often where most companies get absent-minded. To build a business, we all go overboard to please, so remember not to cut any corners to retain or maintain your company's integrity.

Making An Impression

Maintaining a polite, professional presence over the phone is the first step toward making a positive impression on the person on the other end. By effectively using your voice, words, and even the tone of your voice, you can gain a caller's trust – and get down to business.

Here are some tips to help you do just that:

VOICE:

- Speak clearly and at a good volume – don't mumble or whisper.
- Speak carefully – don't rush or confuse yourself.
- Enunciate properly – don't let your words be misheard or misunderstood.

WORDS:

- Use simple words that anyone can understand.
- Avoid technical terms and slang.

- Avoid long, drawn-out sentences – give complete information, but get to the point, remember, being pleasant is a MUST.

TONE:

- Keep a friendly and level voice. Maintain a constant cadence when speaking.
- Being helpful and understanding – sound eager to solve the caller's issue or issues.
- Be calm and confident – remember you are the professional.
- Never be abrupt or rude – even if the client is rude or abrupt with you.

THE GOLDEN RULE

When placing a call:

1. Have a purpose to your call. Make sure you have the training or a corporate script to support your purpose.
2. Be positive. Even if your call is for collection of a debt, medical reasons, or sale of a product or service.
3. Place the call at an appropriate time, these times will vary depending on the industry. Never make calls to a customer when they obviously cannot take your call.
4. Keep conversations short. Always engage the customer.
5. Leave a message only on the second call.
6. Leave coherent messages. Speak slowly and clearly so that your call-back number can be understood.
7. Always end the conversation with the customer on a high note.
8. Use speaker phones in a private setting to maintain customer privacy and avoid being interrupted.
9. Try to accomplish important calls in the morning to give customers time to return your call.

Think about it – you would not like being treated poorly over the telephone, so why would anyone else? When handling customer service calls, always remember to treat the consumer as if *you* were the customer.

Here are a few guidelines for putting that rule into practice:

GIVE A WARM WELCOME

1. Be prepared to deliver a friendly greeting every time you pick up the telephone. It's best to start by introducing yourself and, if appropriate, the name of your department. Don't be too informal – give a proper greeting, such as, "Good morning, this is (John or Jane)," or "Hello, this is (John or Jane)" (*not* "John or Jane speaking.")

2. Don't hold your mouthpiece too close to your mouth or too far away. Make sure the person has the opportunity to hear you clearly. Never eat food or chew gum over the telephone.

3. Don't let the telephone ring more than three times, even if it means putting the person you're talking to on hold.

BE A PROBLEM SOLVER

- Listen carefully to the caller – make sure you understand what the person needs.
- Be responsible – if you can solve the concern yourself, do so; if not, put him or her in touch with someone who can.
- Be honest – don't make promises you can't keep.
- Be prepared – know where in your company to send incoming calls.

BE POLITE

- Use "please," "thank-you," "I'm sorry," "excuse me" and "good-bye."
- Never leave a caller feeling ignored.
- Be discreet and tactful. Regardless of how the caller acts, it's your responsibility to create a positive image for the company. In a conversation with a customer, always take the high road!

TAKING A MESSAGE

If the person the caller needs to speak to is unavailable, you'll have to take a message. There are two ways you can do this; write down a message yourself or put the caller through to voicemail. Both options require a little bit of care to make sure the customer's message gets to the right person:

- Ask the caller whether he or she would like to leave a message or be placed in the voicemail system. NEVER ASSUME!

- When taking a message, be sure to get the caller's important information:

  1. His or her name

  2. Telephone number

  3. The purpose of the call

  4. The time the call came in and the time the caller will be available for a return call.

REVIEW YOUR COMMUNICATION SKILLS

1. Messages are the most easily understood when:
   a. You use your full command of the language.
   b. They are delivered in terms the receiver will understand.

2. Complex information is more easily understood when you:
   a. Improve clarity by using specific examples and analogies.
   b. Tell the listener to pay careful attention.

3. Key concepts are better remembered when you:
   a. Use repetition to reinforce them.
   b. Express yourself clearly.

4. Organizing a message before transmitting it:
   a. Often takes more time than it is worth.
   b. Makes it easier to understand.

5. The customer service representative can determine the caller's understanding by:

   a. Asking if he or she understands.

   b. Asking the caller to repeat what he or she heard.

6. Listening is more effective when you:

   a. Concentrate on the caller and on what is being said.

   b. Anticipate what the caller is going to say.

7. Understanding is easier when you:

   a. Suspend judgment until the caller finishes the message.

   b. Assume you know the caller's position and judge accordingly.

8. Understanding can be improved by the listener:

   a. Periodically paraphrasing the message back to the caller.

   b. Interrupting to express feelings and emotions.

9. Good listeners:

   a. Have their response ready when the caller stops talking.

   b. Ask questions when they don't understand.

ANSWERS TO THE COMMUNICATION TEST:

1. B

2. A

3. A

4. B

5. B

6. A

7. A

8. A

9. B

STICKY SITUATIONS

When calls don't go as you (or the caller) planned, you need to be prepared to take the proper action. Here are a few situations that can present problems – and how you can effectively handle them.

➤ The customer is raging after a service call from one of your representatives; however, you don't pass the call to a supervisor or manager. The first five to ten minutes of any problem call will determine whether you can handle the call or whether you should pass the call to a tier 2 or the escalation team of your company.

➤ Not all customer service calls go badly, but when they occur, we're on guard for the next 10 service calls made. It boils down to the following expectations: When we as the consumer call customer service, we often know what our needs are and we want to hear "yes" when calling for service. We don't want to hear "tomorrow" or "hold on," or "I'll transfer you," and we don't want to be rushed. When that happens, we get highly upset, because we feel customer service means "Fix it, NOW!"

THE BOUNCE

A caller's situation builds quickly if he or she keeps getting the "bureaucratic bounce" or is transferred to multiple representatives. The caller feels like the buck is being passed. The best way to stop the "bouncing" call is to take responsibility and settle the issue yourself.

Here are a few tips on how to handle the "bounce":

1. Be understanding – sympathize with the caller's plight.

2. Take responsibility for getting an answer.

3. Start from the beginning – ask the questions that will help solve the problem.

4. If you can't help the caller, take down his or her name and number and assure him or her that you'll call back as soon as you DO have the answer. The next 24 hours would be appropriate.

5. If you transfer the call to someone else, send along the caller's name and situation and make sure the person receiving the call can be of help.

6. Don't send the caller off on another series
   of transfers – stay on the line with the person
   until you've found someone who can offer
   a solution.

HOLDING PATTERNS

Equally annoying for a caller is the command to "Please hold." Most business callers don't have much time in the first place, and if they don't know how long they're going to have to wait, they can feel like they're in limbo.

Don't let callers on hold feel neglected; follow these steps to let them know their call is important:

- Give the caller a choice – and listen to his or her answer. If the person doesn't want to hold, ask if you can take down a brief message instead.

- Give the caller more information. Say something like, "Please hold while I connect you," or, "Can you hold while I ring his office?"

- If the person the caller needs is away from his or her desk, be discreet. Instead of saying, "He's in the bathroom," say, "He's away from his desk at the moment. Would you like to hold OR leave a message or voicemail?"

- Don't keep someone on hold for more than 60 seconds. If you have to, check in on the caller occasionally to let him or her know you're still working on putting the call through.

■ While you shouldn't overuse it, the holding option is always better than laying the phone on the desk or putting your hand over the mouthpiece. The caller shouldn't hear your office conversations and noise in the background while holding.

THE MYSTERY CALLER

You know who this person is – the one who refuses to leave a message but claims he or she will "call back." Don't leave it to chance; in the business world, missed calls are missed opportunities.

- Ask for a name and number – reassure the caller that the person needed will call back.
- Ask if someone else in the office can help. Emphasize that you and others are willing to assist the caller.

KEEP YOUR COOL

It's 4:45 p.m., you've had a terrible day, and you just had the caller from your nightmares on the line – a perfect excuse to unleash your pent-up frustration on the next caller, right? Before you do, remember that losing your composure over the phone can cost you – and your company – valuable business and goodwill.

Instead of blowing your cool, keep these steps in mind to get through that next call:

- Take a few seconds – pause long enough to separate yourself from the angering situation.
- Take a breath to help shift gears emotionally.
- Compose yourself – look at the next call as a chance to get off on a better foot.
- Think of something funny – a smile on your face will actually bring a "smile" to your voice.
- Then answer the call.

THE FIXER

Every complaint starts out the same – the caller is not happy, and you're being asked for answers. If you handle the call poorly, you've gotten nowhere – and have possibly lost a client. If you take these steps to fix the situation, however, you can turn a critic into a fan:

Don't take it personally – think of the call as a request for assistance. You're being given a chance to make things right.

- Side with the caller – acknowledge that there is a problem, regardless of whether it's your or your company's fault.
- Ask questions – be sure you understand what the problem is before you try to fix it.
- Don't give arguments or excuses – the caller doesn't want them, and you're not going to solve anything by making them.
- Fix the problem. If you can't do it, put the person in touch with someone who can. The key is to assure the caller that steps are being taken to address his or her needs.

MULTI-TASKING

You're on the phone with a customer, and then your other line starts ringing. And then your *other* lines ring. Whatever you do, don't fail to answer. Your time is valuable, and so is theirs. Follow these guidelines to juggle those calls while getting things done:

- As before, even if you're on the line with someone else, don't let the phone ring more than three times. Ask the current caller if he or she can hold, then pick up the ringing line.

- Give long-distance calls priority over local calls. However, all calls are important.

- Don't keep callers on hold for too long – and don't forget about anyone who is waiting.

- In addition to asking callers to hold, ask them if they would rather leave a message or have you call them right back.

Here's a question I got from someone on the subject of multi-tasking:

E-Diva:

I have been working for a company for 10 years and my boss just informed me six months ago that I am not good at multi-tasking. I am completing my work with accuracy, but because of the amount of work assigned, I find myself working overtime just to keep up. What exactly is multi-tasking? What can you suggest to minimize my overtime?

Mr. Over-Worked/Stressed

෧෬

My response was:

Dear Mr. Over-Worked/Stressed:

I regret to hear that your company of 10 years is just now talking about multi-tasking. Most of us multi-task already, but the phenomenon is now considered a necessity. With fewer workers and less money due to downsizing, companies are asking their workers to take on more duties and responsibilities.

Multi-tasking means handling two or more tasks at one time without dropping the ball. For some of us, this is an everyday fact of life. For example, working women who have children handle their children's

after-school activities, cook their family's meals, make sure that their husband's new suit is picked up from the tailor, as well as making sure that their pre-sentation is ready for tomorrow morning's meeting. This is a normal picture of a working woman – and of my days as a young mother.

There are many pros and cons on multi-tasking. The PROS:

1. Keeps most people energized and mentally stimulated.

2. Keeps jobs from getting boring.

3. Within a project link, your computer can show: folder, application, URL address, single document, PowerPoint, mind map, etc. – with just a touch of the keys.

4. The use of Outlook, MS Project, and other programs enables projects to be mixed together for fast changes and juggling of projects.

The CONS:

1. Multi-tasking makes some people less efficient.

2. Reduces the level of brainpower used for each task.

3. Can produce or aggravate stress.

4. Time can be lost switching from task to task.

In a study published in the *Journal of Experimental Psychology*, it was shown that the mind slows down when it switches back and forth between tasks. The only way to alleviate this problem is to put more time, even just a few seconds, between tasks. A second study, published in *NeuroImage*, also notes that the mind does not cope well with multi-tasking. Even when tasks used different parts of the brain, visual input dropped 29 percent and listening success fell 53 percent. These studies reported that when people have to do too many things at once, additional worry can build, creating a stress response. The adrenaline rush can damage the cells that form new memories.

SCREENING CALLS

Sometimes an executive will tell you to hold all calls, or only let important ones through. This puts you in the precarious position of having to screen calls. Figuring out who is calling (and why) without offending the caller requires tact and discretion. This is not always easy to do when – according to your boss, at least – the call may not be important enough to take. Here are some suggestions to help you:

- Find out who is calling. Don't be blunt: use a sensitive or neutral phrase such as, "May I ask who is calling?"

- If you can't put the person through, be honest but discreet – say something like, "Mr. Smith is in conference right now. Can he call you back this afternoon?" or, "Mrs. Jones can't take your call at the moment. Can she return your call later?"

- Ask for a specific time when your boss can call the person back. This reassures the caller that he or she is not being rejected.

Always Remember These Points:

- Introduce yourself.
- Keep a "smile" in your voice.
- Be polite and professional.
- Be ready to serve the caller.
- Be prepared.

This was a question an employee asked me with regard to quality service:

E-Diva:

I'm a sales representative. I have asked my manager over and over again, "How do we know our clients are satisfied?" but he can't seem to tell me. How do you handle excellent quality when it comes to customer service?

Mr. Service

⚭

My response to the employee:

Dear Mr. Service:

A wise, long-tenured veteran business owner in the Executive Search business once said to me, "E-Diva, our business can be very complex, yet

at its heart, it's very simple. Always KISS [Keep It Simple, Stupid]: It's all about serving clients."

Think for a minute about the service professionals in your life: your doctor, your lawyer, your accountant, your financial advisor, or insurance salesman. How did you initially come to them? Referrals from your family members or friends are always great. Or perhaps the location of the service makes it convenient? Maybe it's the price of the service? You heard from someone that "they are a good business?"

How long have you used their service? Why do you go back to them? Do they meet or exceed your expectations every time?

Early in my career, I had the good fortune to attend a management development program with a Fortune 50 bank – a world-class service company. Many of the classes emphasized service quality. Two Disney-style courses I remember were: "How to Delight Your Clients Every Time" and "The Magic of Customer Service." These programs are still relevant today...

Relevant questions for 2010 are: What can we do to increase the quality of our service? Why not ask our clients – the very people we are serving?

One survey question we asked was, "What can we do to serve you better?" One answer was, "I'd like to be called once in a while when you don't want to sell me something." So, we implemented our Service Quality Calling Program. On a consistent basis, our customer service representatives send e-mails to our existing clients, and e-mails or cards are sent to perspective clients. Our relationship managers call quarterly to ask, "Is there anything we can do to assist you?" The response is often, "Not now, but thanks for calling."

The results: We developed a positive service quality reputation that led to measurable, increased client retention and new business. New and retained business equals job security.

Create a client satisfaction survey, written or verbal, and ask your clients how they want to be served. The best ideas can come from your current clients. Or call some of your larger businesses that have a customer satisfaction survey for ideas to tweak your business. Most businesses have an industry standard.

Those who have seen my training know that I emphasize why it is so important to be a consultant to our clients. The same approach is closely tied to how we serve them. Thinking like a consultant, let's ask the following service-quality questions from our clients' perspective:

What do our clients expect from us?

- *Being available when they call us.*
- *A can-do communication style.*
- *Qualified candidates.*
- *Reasonably fast service.*
- *Competitive pricing.*

What can we offer our clients that will exceed their expectations?

- *A trusting, open relationship*
- *Anticipation of their needs.*
- *Industry-specific market knowledge.*
- *Our advice, counsel,*
  and/or recommendations.
- *Referring top-tier candidates in less*
  time than we said we would.

To exceed client expectations, we need to deliver what we said we would in the time frame we promised at the outset.

Eight KISS Service Quality Ideas:

1- Communicate with your clients consistently, on a regular basis, by phone and/or e-mail. My firm sends a valued-added e-mail to our industry-specific client segments on a quarterly basis.

2- Send a personal note or article you thought a client would be interested in. Even if they're not, they'll appreciate your thought.

3- Take your client to lunch – or a sporting event or a concert – for no reason other than to get to know them better. Or send them the tickets!

4- Send holiday cards. An e-card can be fast and cost-effective.

5- Tell your client a memorable story. Laugh with them.

6- Share industry-specific knowledge that will help them "look good" internally.

7- From your conversations, identify their needs; i.e. to fill an open position and call with a qualified and motivated top candidate.

8- As highlighted above, create a client satisfaction survey designed to ask your clients how you can increase your service quality.

Ideas for service quality tracking are:

➤Track and retain phone calls and/ or letters received from clients commending service quality.

➤ Client satisfaction survey scores.

➢ Track and/or record service quality calls.
➢ Implement service quality awards – monthly and annually.
➢ Your idea: _____.
➢ Your client's idea: _____.

In summary, by taking simple steps to increase your service quality, you can significantly increase your firm's repeat business – and keep your clients coming back. The time to implement such programs is now! New clients are calling daily.

> *"Never underestimate the power of a kind word or deed."*
> **– Anonymous**

Customer Service Questions

Q. *Are more companies moving toward automated call centers?*

A. No, just the opposite. More and more companies are returning to the U.S. with call centers focusing on customer satisfaction. The human touch is important to many service companies, banks, insurance companies, and even state and federal government offices.

However, automated systems can be done well or done poorly. FedEx, for instance, receives 65,000 customer service calls a day and cannot have a human being answer all those calls. But even with automation, its agents average 100 to 200 phone calls *each* per eight-hour shift. The key to making automation work is to balance the technology with humanity—companies have to make it possible to reach a human being relatively easily, because when we call customer service, we've usually exhausted other options.

E-Diva:

My company assisted in building a home last year and the window screens in the home's Florida room were warped. Since we provided the service to the homeowner, we vowed to replace them; our company sent a representative to take the window screens out to be replaced. It's been eight months and we forgot to bring back the replacements. Should we call the person and say we forgot?

Upset and Surprised

∾

Dear Upset and Surprised Customer:

In writing this guide, I realized that most companies don't intend to give bad service; however, consumers must do our part and work with the companies we asked for service. As a business owner I can count on one hand how many times I forgot to call a customer to follow up on a project, but it happens.

I would suggest you call from the service department and explain what happened. If you still have a problem getting this matter resolved, ask for the Manager.

Assume the honest approach works.

What the world needs are more friendly business relationships with customers. Being honest with customers should be at the top of your list. Simply explain what happened – the order was misplaced or you failed to follow up – and offer a discount on their next service.

E- Diva:

I actually have a great story to share. We have a service for snow removal and lawn maintenance that we've used for three years. We were approached by a neighbor, who offered to remove our snow for free, so we accepted; however, after two months of not getting the stellar service we had become accustomed to, I had to call the lawn service to come back.

What I remembered is that the lawn service came back and added additional services like shoveling the sidewalks and shoveling the stairway by hand. The best part is, the fee was not increased from the year before.

Speaking of customer service, this company calls all the time to ask if there is anything else they can do for me and my husband. We are extremely happy! This is real CUSTOMER SERVICE!

Hey, Diva:

Do you advise people with customer service jobs to take classes? Or do you think on-the-job training is better?

CSR Associate

∽

Dear CSR Associate:

If you're going to be a lifelong learner and educator, it's important to always refine your craft. Learning the job while working would be my first choice, and the reason I suggest it is because every line of business is different: the service, products, lingo, acronyms, statistics, etc.

However, any classes in customer service that cover such topics as how to deal with customer dissatisfaction, the customer is always right, and how to help people in this economy who are stressed, can all help when you are dealing with the human element. Providing customer service means working with an array of human emotions daily.

Remember, gratitude is the heart's memory. And good customers are hard to find, so let's keep them happy!

∽

Another question from a client:

E-Diva:

I am a manager and my company is having problems in finding out if our customer service teams are working effectively. What would be some great tools for us?

Mr. Manager

༂

To answer your question, Mr. Manager:

Based on the type of call center you run for customer service (inbound customer services, outbound sales, tech support, collections, etc.) and the data available to establish a standard for your teams, you must measure two levels of effectiveness: the overall call-center level and the individual representative's level.

At a call-center level I'd like to see overall performance for customer satisfaction (surveys), first call resolution (via a measured survey or data analysis) and call transfers, along with on-hold times for the customers calling in to your establishment. The need to balance quality with the "cost" of quality is difficult. Establish a standard in the context of your budget with the efficiency of your team's skills and abilities.

The CSR's level of quality from a level of audited recorded calls, transfer rates, and on-hold times MUST be measured.

If you don't have someone on your team who can handle this level of management, contract with an outside management team to coach or otherwise help with raising your levels of scoring to achieve your needed goals.

I strongly believe that customer satisfaction surveys are always the best idea.

Finally, as a manager you must include in your measurement tool each individual's level of enthusiasm, engagement, empathy, and technical competency. We employers can lose some of the best talent by not looking at all factors. Coaching and training is our job...

FINAL POINTS

The following information is from THE UNITED STATES Bureau of Labor Statistics – Department Of Labor- www.bls.gov

Customer service representatives are expected to experience <u>faster than average</u> growth. Furthermore, job prospects should be <u>good</u> as many workers who leave this very large occupation will need to be replaced.

Employment change. Employment of customer service representatives is expected to grow by about 18 percent over the 2008-18 period, faster than the average for all occupations. Providing quality customer service is important to nearly every company in the economy; in addition, companies are expected to place increasing emphasis on customer relationships, resulting in increased demand for customer service representatives. This very large occupation is projected to provide about 400,000 new jobs over the next decade.

Customer service representatives are especially prevalent in the finance and insurance industry, as many customer interactions do not require physical contact. Employment of customer service representatives in this industry is expected to increase 9 percent over the 2008-18 period.

Although technology has tempered growth of this occupation to some degree, it has also created many opportunities for growth. For instance, online banking has reduced the need for telephone banking services. At the same time, however, it has increased the need for customer service representatives who assist users with banking Web sites. Additionally, online services create many new opportunities for customer support representatives as companies that operate on the Internet provide customer service by telephone.

In the past, many companies chose to relocate their customer service call centers in foreign countries, which led to layoffs in some industries. Although many companies continue to offshore some of their customer service jobs, this is becoming less prevalent than in the past. While it continues to be less expensive to hire workers overseas, many companies have found that foreign workers do not have the same cultural sensitivity as those located within the United States.

Job prospects. Prospects for obtaining a job in this field are expected to be good, with more job openings than jobseekers. In particular, bilingual jobseekers should enjoy excellent opportunities. Rapid job growth, coupled with a large number of workers who leave the occupation each year, should make finding a job as a customer service representative relatively easy.

While jobs in some industries may be affected by economic downturns, customer service representatives are not as vulnerable to layoffs as some other workers. This is, in part, because many customer service representatives work in industries where customers have accounts. While customers may have less money to spend, and as a result may choose to purchase fewer goods or services, they continue to have customer service needs. For instance, during an economic downturn, individuals may have less money in their bank accounts, but they continue to need banking services and customer service from their banks. Nevertheless, companies do attempt to cut costs during such times, so downsizing is still a possibility.

National Employment Matrix

Projections data from the National Employment Matrix

Occupational Title	SOC Code	Employment, 2008	Projected Employment, 2018	Change, 2008-18	
				Number	Percent
Customer service representatives	43-4051	2,252,400	2,651,900	399,500	18

NOTE: Data in this table are rounded. See the discussion of the employment projections table in the *Handbook* introductory chapter on *Occupational Information Included in the Handbook*.

SOC means Standard Occupational Classification System.

Earnings About this section

In May 2008, median hourly wages of customer service representatives were $14.36. The middle 50 percent earned between $11.34 and $18.27. The lowest 10 percent earned less than $9.15, and the highest 10 percent earned more than $23.24.

Earnings for customer service representatives vary according to level of skill required, experience, training, location, and size of firm. Median hourly wages in the industries employing the largest numbers of these workers in May 2008 were:

Insurance carriers	$15.74
Agencies, brokerages, and other insurance related activities	$15.28
Depository credit intermediation	$14.56
Employment services	$12.73
Business support services	$11.56

In addition to receiving an hourly wage, full-time customer service representatives who work evenings, nights, weekends, or holidays may receive shift differential pay. Also, because call centers are often open during extended hours, or even 24 hours a day, some customer service representatives have the benefit of being able to work a schedule that does not conform to the traditional workweek. Other benefits can include life and health insurance, pensions, bonuses, employer-provided training, and discounts on the products and services the company offers.

∽

Let's put the value back in one on one human interaction. I hope these points of reference will assist you in your successful quest for *"CUSTOMER SERVICE! RECOGNIZING, EDUCATING, AND PROMOTING."*

Dr. Rae Pearson (E-Diva)

www.ingramcontent.com/pod-product-compliance
Lightning Source LLC
Chambersburg PA
CBHW021924170526
45157CB00005B/2180